This book belongs to

_____

I am _____ like Mom!

For my kids — Makena, Hallie, and Kaden;
And to Phil — thanks for always cheering me on!
- AS

For Chris and our munchkins, Emma and Ezra!
- AB

And for all the mamas (including our own!) who inspire us everyday.

First Edition June 2019
Book design by Aubrey Boyer
ISBN: 9780578529073

www.iamstronglikemom.com

I am STRONG like Mom

Written by Alyssa Serchia
Illustrated by Aubrey Boyer

Dear Mamas,
In your kids' eyes, you are a superhero.
It doesn't matter if you're "perfect."
It doesn't matter if you can do 20 push-ups or run marathons.
It doesn't matter if you're grumpy some days.
Your kids look at you and see someone amazing.
Someone strong.
Someone who loves them. Someone they love. You have the
hardest job in the world, Mamas.
And you're doing *awesome*.

 Alyssa

My mom is really fun.
I like to laugh too!

I am **Happy** like Mom.

My mom believes in herself.
I'm pretty awesome too!

I am Confident like Mom.

My mom shares so much love.
I treat my friends with kindness too!

I am **Kind** like Mom.

My mom has rough days.
I have worries and tears too!

My mom creates beautiful things.
I like to make stuff too!

I am
CREATIVE
like Mom.

My mom likes to run.
I have super speed too!

I am **FAST** like Mom.

My mom does things that scare her.
I like to try new things too!

I am **BRAVE** like Mom.

My mom waits for me a lot.
I am learning to wait for the things I want too!

I am **patient** like Mom.

My mom never gives up.
I always keep trying too!

I am **PERSISTENT** like Mom.

My mom can do hard things.
I can do things that are difficult for me too!

I am STRONG like Mom.

My mom climbs high.
I can reach for the stars too!

About the Author

Alyssa and her husband have three little kiddos and she is a fitness coach for moms and kids. She loves to hike in the mountains, play at the beach, and do almost anything outside!
You can often find Alyssa handstanding in random locations, running with at least two kids in her jogger, or impatiently waiting for her gluten-free chocolate chip cookies to bake.
She hopes to empower the next generation to be strong, kind, and to never give up on their dreams!

About the Illustrator

Aubrey and her husband have two little kids and live wherever the military takes them. She is a designer and illustrator who loves to draw, and is always creating with her kids. The beach is her happy place, and you can usually find her with a coffee in one hand and art supplies or a book in the other.

Fun Fact!

Alyssa and Aubrey are SISTERS!
They live far apart but when they get together, they spend their time drinking coffee, laughing, going for walks, and chasing all of their tiny little humans.
The kids in this book are inspired by a combination of all five of Alyssa and Aubrey's kids.

CPSIA information can be obtained
at www.ICGtesting.com
Printed in the USA
LVHW070510050819
626516LV00024B/393/P